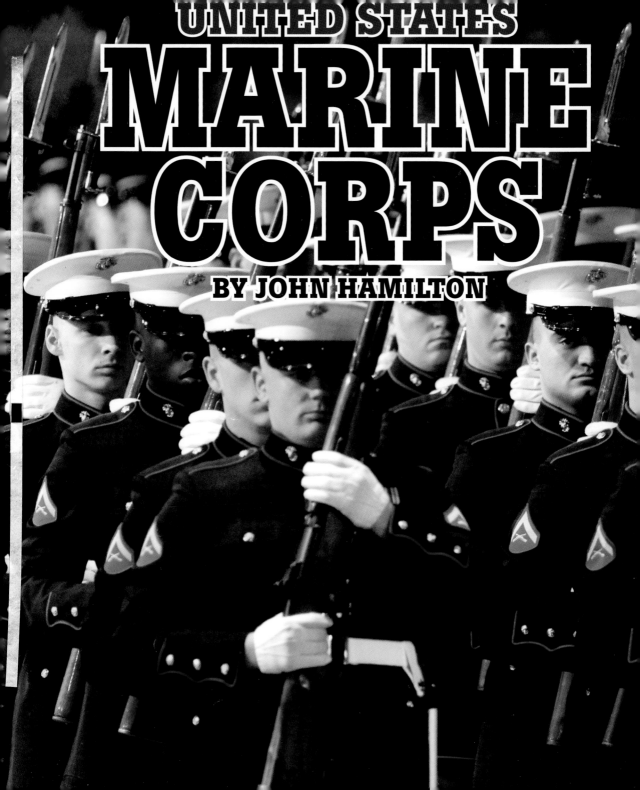

UNITED STATES
MARINE CORPS

BY JOHN HAMILTON

VISIT US AT
WWW.ABDOPUBLISHING.COM

Published by ABDO Publishing Company, 8000 West 78th Street, Suite 310, Edina, MN 55439. Copyright ©2012 by Abdo Consulting Group, Inc. International copyrights reserved in all countries. No part of this book may be reproduced in any form without written permission from the publisher. A&D Xtreme™ is a trademark and logo of ABDO Publishing Company.

Printed in the United States of America, North Mankato, Minnesota.
052011
092011

 PRINTED ON RECYCLED PAPER

Editor: Sue Hamilton
Graphic Design: Sue Hamilton
Cover Design: John Hamilton
Cover Photo: U.S. Marine Corps
Interior Photos: AP-pgs 8-10; Corbis-pgs 26-27; C.H. Waterhouse-pg 8 (insert); Dept of Defense-pgs 12 (insert) & 32; Defense Video & Imagery Distribution System (DVIDS)-20-22, 24-25, 30 & 31; Photospin-pg 16; United States Marine Corps-pgs 1-7, 11-15, 17-19, 23, 24 (insert), 28 & 29.

Library of Congress Cataloging-in-Publication Data

Hamilton, John, 1959-
United States Marine Corps / John Hamilton.
    p. cm. -- (United States armed forces)
Includes index.
ISBN 978-1-61783-070-9
1. United States. Marine Corps--Juvenile literature. I. Title.
VE23.H293 2012
359.9'60973--dc23
                                            2011018116

CONTENTS

THE UNITED STATES MARINE CORPS

The United States Marine Corps is an all-purpose military force that mobilizes quickly and strikes aggressively. Marines are elite fighters. They can be deployed quickly almost anywhere in the world. The Marine Corps can protect United States interests wherever a crisis flares.

XTREME FACT
A famous Marine Corps motto is "First to Fight."

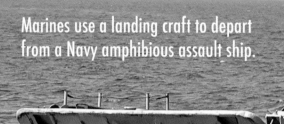

Marines use a landing craft to depart from a Navy amphibious assault ship.

The Marine Corps is part of the Department of the Navy. However, even though it works closely with the Navy, the Marine Corps is a separate branch of the armed services.

The United States Marine Corps is smaller than the U.S. Army, Navy, or Air Force. As of 2011, there are about 201,000 Marines on active duty, with an additional 40,000 reserves.

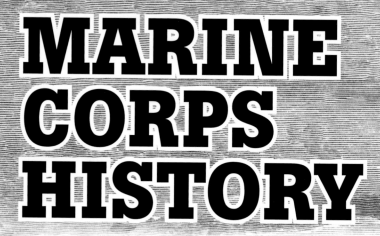

MARINE CORPS HISTORY

The United States Marine Corps was created by the Continental Congress on November 10, 1775, during the Revolutionary War. Marines served aboard Continental Navy ships to protect them.

Marines fighting Barbary pirates in Tripoli in 1805.

The Marines also used amphibious assaults on ground targets, attacking enemy ports, bases, and cities from the sea. In 1805, Marines fought Barbary pirates and captured the North African city of Derna, Tripoli. And in 1847, during the Mexican-American War, Marines were among the first troops to enter the enemy's capital of Mexico City.

United States troops landed at Veracruz, Mexico, during the Mexican-American War in 1847.

In World War I, the Marines earned their tough reputation at the Battle of Belleau Wood in France. During World War II, the Marines launched many amphibious assaults against Japanese forces in the Pacific, including battles at Guadalcanal, Iwo Jima, and Okinawa. Marines also played important roles in the Korean and Vietnam Wars.

U.S. Marines raise the American flag on Iwo Jima, on February 23, 1945. The island, south of Japan, was the site of one of the bloodiest battles of World War II.

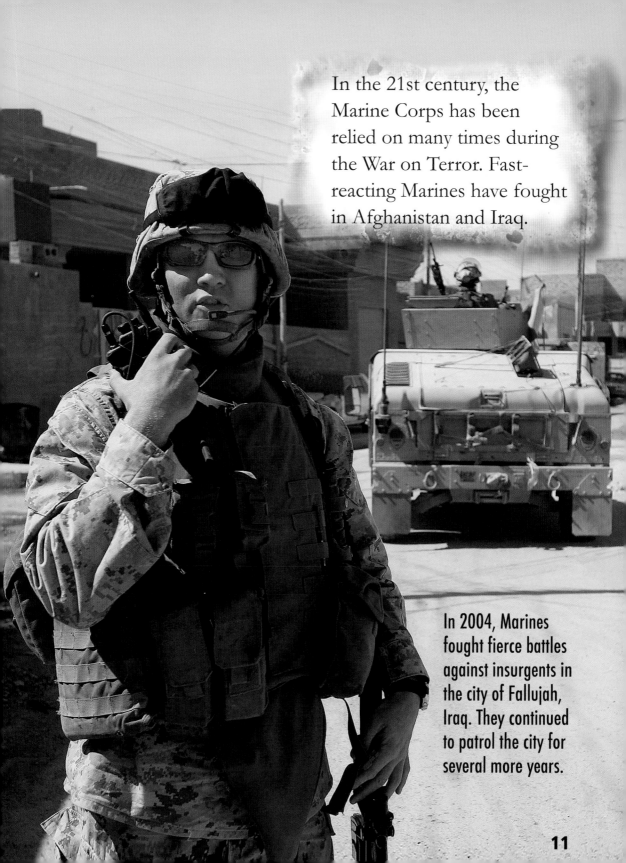

In the 21st century, the Marine Corps has been relied on many times during the War on Terror. Fast-reacting Marines have fought in Afghanistan and Iraq.

In 2004, Marines fought fierce battles against insurgents in the city of Fallujah, Iraq. They continued to patrol the city for several more years.

MARINE TRAINING

Marines receive training from a drill instructor.

A Marine undergoes an endurance test.

Men and women between 17 and 29 can enlist in the Marine Corps. Recruits undergo 13 weeks of intense training, called boot camp, at recruit depots in either San Diego, California, or Parris Island, South Carolina. Recruits become physically fit, receive combat training, and learn how to take orders. Leadership skills are also highly valued.

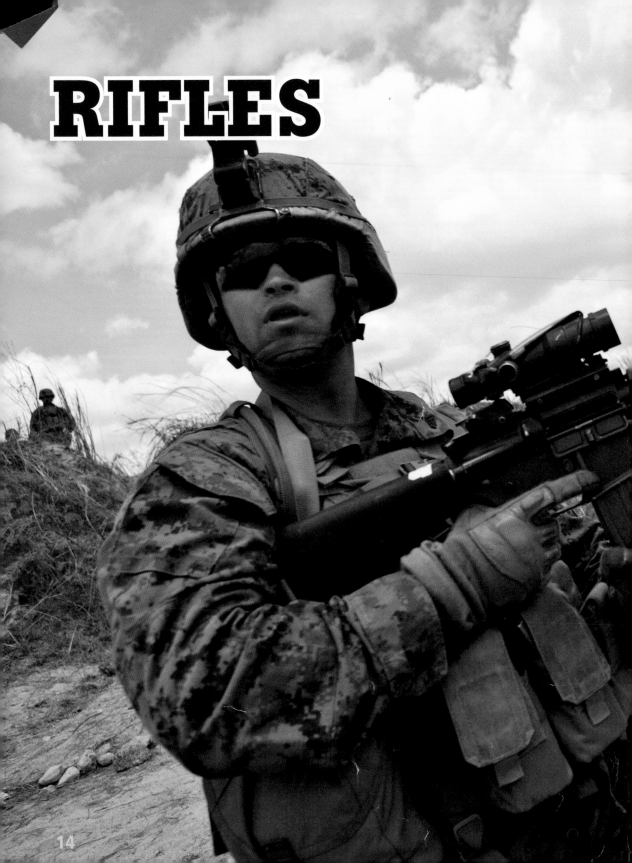

RIFLES

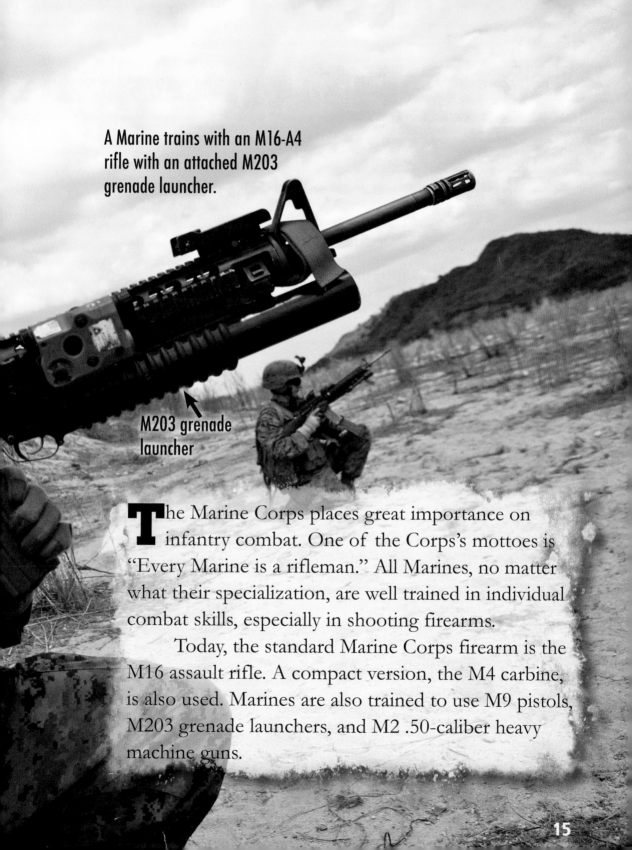

A Marine trains with an M16-A4 rifle with an attached M203 grenade launcher.

M203 grenade launcher

The Marine Corps places great importance on infantry combat. One of the Corps's mottoes is "Every Marine is a rifleman." All Marines, no matter what their specialization, are well trained in individual combat skills, especially in shooting firearms.

Today, the standard Marine Corps firearm is the M16 assault rifle. A compact version, the M4 carbine, is also used. Marines are also trained to use M9 pistols, M203 grenade launchers, and M2 .50-caliber heavy machine guns.

AMPHIBIOUS ASSAULT

Marines are famous for their skill in amphibious assault, attacking land targets from the sea.

 XTREME FACT
Marines used to wear leather collars as part of their uniform. That is how they earned the nickname "leathernecks."

Marines use the Navy's mobility to get them close to combat zones, then forcefully enter enemy territory using amphibious assault vehicles and support aircraft.

In a training exercise, an AH-1W Super Cobra helicopter provides air support to a Marine amphibious assault landing on a beach in Egypt.

The Marine Corps's AAV-7 Amphibious Assault Vehicle (AAV) is a fully tracked, lightly armored vehicle that travels through water and overland. It can transport 21 combat-equipped Marines or 10,000 pounds (4,536 kg) of cargo.

XTREME FACT
On land, the AAV-7 can travel up to 400 miles (644 km) inland at highway speeds up to 45 miles per hour (72 kph).

ARMOR

The Marine Corps uses a variation of the U.S. Army's M1 Abrams main battle tank. It is a highly mobile, heavily armored tracked vehicle. Shells fired from the Abrams's 120mm smoothbore cannon can easily destroy most enemy vehicles.

Marines fire an Abrams battle tank's 120mm smoothbore cannon on a live-fire range in Djibouti, Africa.

BATTLE TRANSPORT

Marines are quickly dropped into battle zones by CH-46 Sea Knight helicopters and MV-22 Osprey tilt-rotor aircraft. Heavier equipment is airlifted by CH-53E Super Stallion helicopters.

Two Marines exit a CH-46 Sea Knight helicopter.

A Super Stallion moves a Humvee.

XTREME FACT
Ospreys take off vertically, like helicopters. They can then rotate their propellers and fly like regular airplanes. Ospreys are faster and have a longer range than conventional helicopters.

An MV-22 Osprey aircraft lifts a 7,000-pound (3,175-kg) howitzer.

ATTACK AIRCRAFT

Marine attack aircraft are used to support troops on the ground. This tactic is called "close air support." Marine pilots fly several kinds of aircraft. The F/A-18 Hornet carries precision-guided missiles and bombs. The AV-8B Harrier II can hover in midair or fly nearly at the speed of sound. The AH-1W Super Cobra attack helicopter is highly effective at escorting ground troops and attacking the enemy, day or night.

Two F/A-18 Hornets

AH-1W Super Cobra

An AV-8B Harrier hovers before landing aboard the USS *Bataan*.

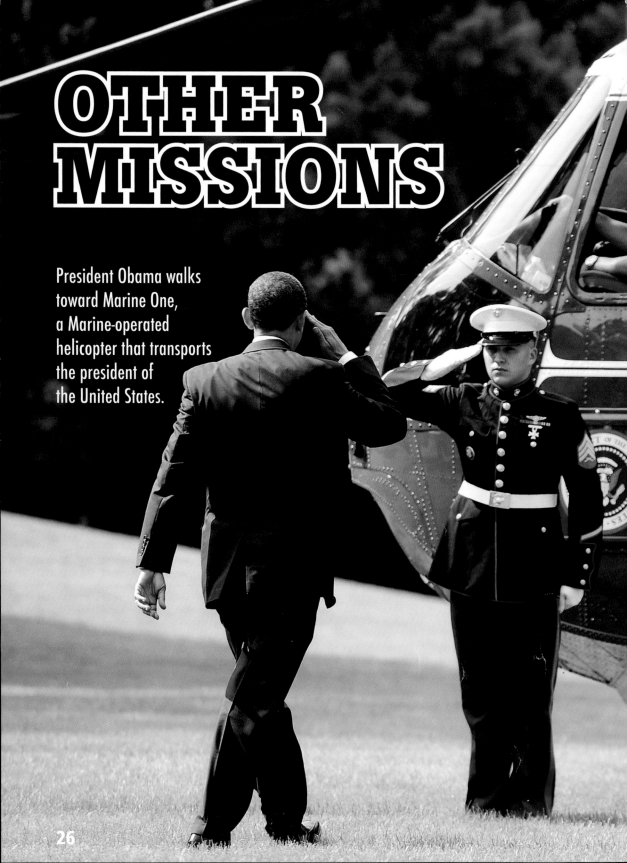

OTHER MISSIONS

President Obama walks toward Marine One, a Marine-operated helicopter that transports the president of the United States.

In addition to their combat duties, Marines also stand guard at the White House and Camp David. In addition, the Marine Embassy Security Command protects U.S. embassies and consulates in more than 140 foreign posts around the world.

THE FUTURE

During its long history, cost-cutting politicians have sometimes threatened to disband the United States Marine Corps. But most people recognize the value of a quick-strike force that can fight anywhere in the world. Modern warfare, especially the War on Terror, requires smaller, faster units that can respond forcefully to future threats. With the best-trained fighters and most advanced technology available, the Marine Corps is prepared for whatever the future holds.

GLOSSARY

AMPHIBIOUS
The ability to live and function in both land and water. The United States Marine Corps specializes in amphibious assaults, attacking from the sea and landing groups of fighters on seashores to seize enemy ports, bases, and other targets.

ASSAULT RIFLE
Assault rifles are the most commonly used weapons used by today's armed forces. They use medium-power cartridges (the part containing the bullet), and are fired from the shoulder. Soldiers can either fire the weapon in semiautomatic mode (one shot or short burst every time the trigger is pulled), or in fully automatic (the weapon fires rapidly until the trigger is released or ammo runs out). The U.S. Marine Corps's main assault rifles are the M16 and M4 carbine.

CAMP DAVID
A place for the current United States president, family, and invited guests to relax. Camp David is located in the Catoctin Mountains of northern Maryland. It is guarded by United States Marines.

COMBAT ZONE
An area where military fighting takes place.

CONTINENTAL CONGRESS
A group that governed the 13 American colonies during

the Revolutionary War. The Continental Congress issued the American Declaration of Independence in 1776.

REVOLUTIONARY WAR
The war fought between the American colonies and Great Britain from 1775-1783. It is also known as the War of Independence or the American Revolution. America won its independence in the war.

SMOOTHBORE CANNON
A cannon with a smooth interior barrel, instead of spiraled grooves.

SPEED OF SOUND
The speed at which a sound wave travels. In dry air, at a temperature of 68 degrees Fahrenheit (20 degrees Celsius), sound travels at the rate of 1,126 feet per second (343.2 meters per second). This is about one mile in five seconds (one kilometer in three seconds).

VIETNAM WAR
A conflict between the countries of North Vietnam and South Vietnam from 1955-1975. Communist North Vietnam was supported by China and the Soviet Union. The United States entered the war on the side of South Vietnam.

WAR ON TERROR
An international effort, led by the United States and the United Kingdom, to eliminate terrorist groups such as al-Qaeda, in countries such as Afghanistan, Philippines, and Iraq.

INDEX